Inspiring
Women
Every Day

May

WATER OF LIFE
....
ELEANOR HEWETT

June

MY TIMES,
GOD'S TIMING
....
CAROL HERZIG

Plus ... Special Article, Ministry Report and CWR Events Page

MIX
Paper from
responsible sources
FSC® C015900

ELEANOR HEWETT

Eleanor Hewett has worked for many charities, including Scope and Care International. She spent two years working with people living with HIV/AIDS in Kenya as a Voluntary Service Overseas volunteer. She lives in Cardiff, where she attends Cathays Methodist Church and leads a Women's Bible Study group. Eleanor is blessed by a wonderful family and friends. She loves being a Mum to her two children Alex (four) and Christy (one), and enjoys taking them to the park or playing in the garden. This is her first time writing for *Inspiring Women Every Day*.

CAROL HERZIG

After teaching Modern Languages for five years (which she loved), Carol Herzig followed God's call to overseas mission by joining World Horizons, where she met her husband, Andrew (a fellow clarinettist and worship team member). Together they worked in inner-city Marseille until Carol was forced to return to the UK through illness. She continues to have overseas mission on her heart – and a passion for worship, unity and learning more of God and His ways. In recent years, Carol has worked for Christian charities and has been an editor for CWR since 2006. One unfulfilled desire is to be further involved with children through writing and storytelling.

Water of life

Genesis 1:1–10

'In the beginning
… the Spirit of
God was hovering
over the waters.'
(vv.1–2)

We read of the birth of the world – water is present at the very beginning, before even the light. Just as we humans are born out of the water of the womb, '... the earth was formed out of water and by water' (2 Pet. 3:5). Amniotic fluids protect us for nine months, as God forms us, shapes us and knows us.

In the beginning, there was just a watery jumble, until God took control of it and formed the earth, creating order from chaos. Water became the basis of life – but only as part of God's plan for creation; without God, the water would still be chaos.

At first, the earth was formless and empty. By dividing the waters God gave order to the world. The waters of the earth were separated from the atmospheric waters of the heavens by the dry land – creating oceans, seas, polar ice caps, clouds, rain and rivers. Scientists estimate that 75 per cent of the earth's surface is water-covered, plus the water beneath our feet, deep in the ground. Water is essential to all forms of life, and most definitely to human health. In fact, 72 per cent of the human body is made of water. Although we can go for longer periods without food; human beings can only survive a few days without water.

Water is more than just a necessity of life. It becomes a thing of beauty and wonder when seen in the shape of a rainbow or a snowflake, as dew, mist or hail, as hot springs or geysers, or supporting eco-systems such as coral reefs. Read on in the first chapter of Genesis, where God commands that the water should teem with living creatures: not just fish either, think of whales, dolphins, otters and ducks, to name but a few.

For prayer and reflection

Lord, thank You for bringing us forth out of water. Thank You for the beauty of Your creation and Your ordered plan for our lives.

River of life

'… for the LORD God had not sent rain on the earth …' (v.5)

To begin with, there was only dry dust; no plant life to cover the surface of the earth. No rain had yet fallen.

Our recent dry summers have caused droughts in parts of the UK, with corresponding hose pipe bans. But imagine a world with no water at all – no rains, rivers or streams, no lakes or seas; just dusty desert where little grows.

When I lived in Kenya, water was a precious commodity. Women would carry buckets of water on their heads for back-breaking distances. Even in Nairobi, there were frequent shortages of water, especially clean water for drinking. Any water I did occasionally get through my pipes had to be filtered, boiled for ten minutes, and cooled, before it was fit to drink. I took care not to waste a drop. I rarely used water just the once; instead I could make a pan of water last for boiling vegetables, washing the dishes, before finally using it to flush the loo!

With our growing realisation of climate change, we are becoming increasingly aware of how our actions affect the world that God created for us to live in. We are custodians of the earth, but we do not always give it the loving care we should. One day, fresh water may become so scarce that people may fight wars over it.

In the perfection of Eden, God does not leave the earth or the garden dry. He waters it by causing streams to rise from the earth which become a great river flowing through Eden. Without water, Eden would be a dry, barren place; the plants, animals and people would have soon died, as none of us can survive long without water. But God's garden flourishes; a garden of life and not death.

For prayer and reflection

We are sorry for our carelessness and our destruction of Your world, Lord.

Resolve to do at least one thing to conserve the amount of water you use on a daily basis.

Moses taken **from the water**

Exodus 2:1–10

'I drew him out of the water.' (v.10)

My *NIV Study Bible* says that the phrase 'papyrus basket' contains two words of Egyptian origin. In fact, the word basket is only used in two places in the Bible – here and also for Noah's ark. Just as Noah coated his ark with pitch to keep the water out, so did Moses' mother many years later – to create a vessel offering safety and sanctuary to her precious son.

Moses' basket was a miniature version of the large, seaworthy papyrus boats mentioned in Isaiah 18:2. I once visited Lake Tana in Ethiopia, one of the largest lakes in the world, with waves and winds to match. Whilst there, I actually saw men making boats out of papyrus reeds just as Ethiopian lake dwellers have done for thousands of years; and then sailing them over the choppy waters of Lake Tana – precarious little rafts when faced with the high waves, strong winds and the lurking hippos.

Water in the Bible often symbolises birth; whether the birth of the whole of creation, or of a single tiny baby who needs protection from the wrath of Pharaoh. Floating in his waterborne cradle, Moses is kept safe. His mother outwits the king. The small ark shields her baby and ensures his continued life.

Sometimes we feel that we need the protective space of an ark around us; somewhere to retreat to and to be safe. God drew us out of the water when we were born, to go forth into the big wide world to do His will. However, it is good to return regularly to His sanctuary, to spend quiet time with Him, which will give us the strength and peace to face those choppy waters of life once more.

For prayer and reflection

Take time to be still and enter God's space – your ark. Take refuge in His presence and take time to rest in the Lord. Read Matthew 11:28.

The rainbow in the clouds

Genesis 9:1–17

'Never again will the waters become a flood to destroy all life.' (v.15)

Just as his basket was a safe place for Moses, God offers a means of salvation – an ark – to Noah and his family facing the danger of the flood. Noah walked with God; and God remembered Noah. He went to great efforts to keep him alive and well throughout the days of the storm.

The water of life can easily become the water of destruction. The fearful narrative of Noah's story shows water as both powerful and dangerous. Yet it is a story with an astonishing end and an incredible promise.

Water becomes even more amazing when light shines through it, creating a myriad of colour, a mighty arch sweeping across the sky. Water is naturally colourless but, with the force of light, it blossoms into the radiance of a rainbow.

Clouds tend to be grey and depressing; in contrast a rainbow can lift our spirits. I rejoice whenever I see a rainbow as it causes me to look afresh for God's promise in my life. One of my best memories is driving down the motorway in heavy rain. The sun was shining from behind, creating a continuous archway of rainbows for the duration of my journey.

The most significant part of this story is the fact that God does not just make a covenant with Noah, but with all living creatures on the earth. And that means me and you. So, when grey skies get you down, remember that God offers each and every one of us salvation in the form of Jesus, just as so long ago He gave Noah an ark. Just like Noah, God remembers us and knows us by name. He cares for us and wants to let His love and His light shine through us, transforming our lives into colour, faithfulness, joy and faith.

For prayer and reflection

Lord, I pray that You shine through my life. Transform me with Your love and Your light.

WEEKEND

Time to praise

For reflection: Psalm 104

'O LORD my God, You are very great …
I will sing praise to my God as long as I live.' (v.1,33)

God is great and His creation reflects His glory – enduring forever. God did not stop creating. Night follows day, seasons turn, springs pour water and grass grows.

God has created this living planet for us. The psalmist demonstrates God's loving care for us – grass for our cattle, plants, food and wine to feed us, olive oil to make us glow, bread to let us know God's love in our hearts. God intends us to be nourished physically, emotionally and spiritually. Only He can sustain us, only He can truly satisfy our souls. God gives us only the best He has created.

Doesn't that feel amazing? To be loved so much that God created the whole world … for you.

Last summer, I grew tomato plants in my garden. I faithfully watered and fed the plants, placing them against a warm, sunny wall. I was rewarded with beautiful red fruit, shiny and sweet. Yet, when I reflected on the combination of a tiny seed, soil and water, I might never have guessed it would bring forth such jewels. This is the wonder of God's never-ending creation.

Optional further reading
Psalm 8; Proverbs 8:22–31; Isaiah 40:12–24

Crossing the river

Joshua 3:14–17;
4:23–24

'... the hand of the
LORD is powerful'
(v.24)

**For prayer and
reflection**

**Lord, help me
to act in Your
strength and
power, instead
of struggling on
my own. Thank
You that You are
always with me
and will never
forsake me.**

The River Jordan features many times throughout the Bible. A major river in Palestine, it was of significant importance to the arid lands surrounding it. The Jordan rises above the Sea of Galilee in the north and runs into the Dead Sea in the south.

At the time of the spring harvest, this mighty river was in flood due to spring rains and snow melting on Mount Hermon. It would have been perfectly understandable if the people had been fearful to step into this powerful stretch of water. They could easily have been dragged under the swift current and washed away.

For Joshua, this was the first real challenge of his leadership. The first chapter of this book tells how God called Joshua '... I will be with you; I will never leave you nor forsake you'; and encouraged him to 'be strong and courageous' (Josh. 1:5–6). God gives His people another chance to enter Canaan after many years of wandering in the wilderness. This is a symbolic crossing, as well as a very real crossing of a natural boundary into the promised land.

The water of the Jordan may be powerful, but God's power is far greater than any river He created. Imagine the scene at the edge of the river. This was not just the crossing of a few strong men. Quite the reverse. In fact, 'the whole nation' crossed in just one day. What an amazing sight to have beheld – an enormous caravan of families, mothers with small children, elderly people, all laden with their baggage and probably leading their animals. The ark of the covenant is God's visual presence with His people, as they walk in His power and cross the Jordan in safety.

CWR MINISTRY EVENTS

Please pray for the team

DATE	EVENT	PLACE	PRESENTER(S)
1 May	Bible Discovery Evening Class - Exile and Coming Home	Waverley Abbey House	Philip Greenslade
2 May	Christ Empowered Living	WAH	Mick & Lynette Brooks
10 May	Discovering More about God's Story [Title TBC]	WAH	Philip Greenslade
21 May	Insight Day - Helping Families Heal	WAH	Andre Radmall
28 May-1 June	Introduction to Biblical Care and Counselling	WAH	Angie Coombes, Richard Laws & the CWR Counselling Team
6 June	The God of Love in a World of Suffering	WAH	Michael Baughen
7 June	Managing Your Time	WAH	Andy Peck
14 June	Preaching with Colour	WAH	Andy Peck
22-24 June	Bible Discovery Weekend - Nothing Can Stop the Gospel	WAH	Philip Greenslade
23 June	Caring God's Way	WAH	Mick Brooks & Lynn Penson
27 June	Education ... A Christian Undertaking?	WAH	Robert Jackson
29 June - 1 July	Marriage on Track	WAH	Andrew & Lynn Penson
30 June	Insight Day - Eating Disorders	WAH	Helena Wilkinson

Please also pray for students and tutors on our ongoing **BA in Counselling** programme at Waverley and our **Certificate and Diploma of Christian Counselling** and **MA in Integrative Psychotherapy** held at London School of Theology.

For full details phone 01252 784700, international +44 (0)1252 784700 or see the CWR website for further information www.cwr.org.uk

Jesus calms **the storm**

Mark 4:35–41

'Who is this? Even the wind and the waves obey him!' (v.41)

Over 12 miles long, the Sea of Galilee is an inland sea, a freshwater lake. Situated in a basin surrounded by mountains, it is particularly susceptible to sudden, violent storms.[1] Mark describes how the water was stirred up into high waves, which smacked across the boat, threatening to swamp it.

In 1986, archaeologists discovered an ancient fishing boat near to Capernaum, which was radiocarbon-dated to the first century AD, and is now in a museum in Israel. Made of wood, the boat was over 26 feet in length. Capable of being both rowed and sailed, it would have had a crew of five – four oarsmen and a helmsman to steer – and could have carried cargo or up to ten passengers.[2]

It is probable that Peter's boat would have been of a similar design, with Jesus sleeping on the helmsman's cushion in the stern. At least four of the disciples were experienced fishermen who surely must have encountered these squalls before, but this time they sensed a real danger – loss of the boat and their livelihood; or even loss of life. Like the merchants in Psalm 107, 'in their peril their courage melted away' and their expert seamanship was of no use to them.

In their panic, they wake Jesus for practical reasons – to help bale the water! But they get a lot more than they expected, as He demonstrates His power over the elements of water and air, and calms the storm. In the storms of life, we may sometimes feel that God is sleeping, but we need to call on Him. Not only will He wake up, but He will calm our storms and give us peace and stillness.

For prayer and reflection

When you call to God, do you sometimes not get the answer you expect? Remember – God's will and not our own; God's power and not our own.

[1] *NIV Study Bible* (London: Hodder & Stoughton, 1998) p.1471
[2] Ian Wilson, *Jesus: The Evidence* (London: Weidenfield & Nicolson, 1996) p.81

Jonah's **prayer**

'I remembered you, LORD' (v.7)

'You hurled me into the deep,' says Jonah to God. Maybe he is not just talking about being thrown in at the deep end literally, but also metaphorically. Jonah had run away from what he perceived as too big a task for him – God had sent him to preach against the great city of Nineveh. Possibly Jonah felt overwhelmed, scared, not up for the job – drowning in his emotions.

Now he finds himself literally drowning. His prayer is a scary and very real description of being submerged by the water; being pulled in all directions by powerful currents; being battered and bruised by waves and breakers; being surrounded by deep, dark water, unable to see a way out; being bound by seaweed which threatened to strangle and choke him.

Do you ever sense that life is threatening to engulf you? Maybe, like Jonah, you feel underequipped for and overwhelmed by the task ahead – whatever it might be. You could be facing challenges at work; coping with a relationship breakdown; or struggling to come to terms with changes in your circumstances, such as a move to a new house that does not feel like home. Yesterday, we read how the disciples called on Jesus during the storm. Here, Jonah calls for help and God listens to his cry.

Our God is a God of love and mercy. Yet again we have another example of how He responds when someone calls on Him. Read the rest of the story to see how God doesn't just answer Jonah's call, but also the call of the people of Nineveh. (3:8)

Don't be like Jonah and keep prayer as a last resort!

For prayer and reflection

Lord, help me to feel Your presence, especially when things get on top of me. Don't let me 'go it alone', but be with me always. I call on You!

Jesus walks on water

Matthew
14:22–33

'Truly you are the
Son of God.' (v.33)

H ere in Britain we love to talk about the weather, possibly because it is so changeable that it makes for interesting conversation. Be it sun, rain or snow, our daily weather conditions are one thing we have no control over. The downside of living on the coast as I do, is the propensity for storms and high winds, particularly during the winter months. Combine the two elements of water and wind and you will find bridges closed to traffic and ferries confined to dock.

Over the last few days, we have read of the power of water, and its danger despite its life-sustaining properties. Yet as Jesus walks on the water, He demonstrates God's complete mastery over the elements.

On the occasion of the previous storm, the disciples had questioned, 'Who is this?' (Mark 4:41). This time, there is no questioning and no hesitation. Jesus' disciples recognise His divine power when they acknowledge Him as the Son of God.

Time has elapsed since the first storm, and the disciples have watched their master heal many people, including the paralysed man and those possessed by demons. He has even raised a girl from the dead. The day before, they had witnessed the feeding of five thousand men with just five loaves and two fish. But walking on water is the culmination point, as Jesus transcends the laws of nature. He stills the wind and walks across the sea as if it were dry land.

The disciples have no doubts. They clearly recognise Jesus as the Son of God, but they don't just leave it there. They worship Him accordingly.

For prayer and reflection

Jesus Christ, Son of God. I worship and adore You. I bow down before Your throne in awe and wonder. You are Lord.

Naaman washes **in the Jordan**

2 Kings 5:1–16

'Wash and be cleansed.' (v.13)

Naaman was the commander of the army, a great man, highly-regarded, a victorious, valiant soldier. He sounds amazing, then comes the 'but'. '... But he had leprosy' (v.1). The Hebrew word for leprosy actually referred to any disease affecting the skin. What is clear however, is that this skin disease carried a stigma. It was evident to anyone who set eyes on Naaman. There was no hiding or disguising his affliction. Do you remember the story of Miriam, whose skin was as white as snow with leprosy (Num. 12:10)?

In New Testament times, lepers were seen as ritually unclean and by law had to live separately from the rest of society. Stigma is still attached to infectious diseases today, such as AIDS or TB; people suffer discrimination because of other people's fear, ignorance and prejudice.

I imagine that Naaman had tried many 'cures' for his leprosy, but nothing had worked. So much so that he is prepared to travel some distance to a strange land and to seek the power of an alien god.

We can be sure that if Naaman had washed in the Damascus rivers, he would not have been healed. In fact, the water of the Jordan on its own was not enough to cure Naaman either. Naaman's leprosy was on the outside, but God was more concerned with what was on the inside – his pride, his rage and his arrogance.

Naaman has to learn to do God's will, to be obedient, and ultimately to trust and have faith in God. It is through God's power that he is cleansed of his disease, not through his own power, but by submission to God's plan and will.

For prayer and reflection

'Lord, if you are willing, you can make me clean' (Matt. 8:2). Lord, please cure me of the weaknesses inside me, make me clean and ready to do Your will.

WEEKEND

Time to rest

For reflection: Psalm 23
'He restores my soul.' (v.3)

After a manic week at work, weekends tend to be even more busy, rushing from one thing to the next, trying to cram more in. Women pride themselves on their ability to multi-task – but are we just in danger of overloading and not actually getting anywhere? Work, family commitments, children, church meetings, home – all are pressures of modern living.

I often use Psalm 23 as an image of God's place for me – why don't you do the same? Imagine lying on green grass. Enjoy the warmth of the sun on your skin. Be aware of the pools of water nearby, glistening in the light, fed by gentle streams. Can you hear the calming flow of the spring water as it bubbles over the rocks of the streambed? Gradually you begin to relax, to let the mundane parts of life go. You are able to sink slowly into God's presence. He is the patient Shepherd who waits for you to turn to Him. He wants to restore and refresh your soul.

This weekend, find a quiet space, and take time beside those restful waters to feel God's peace wash over you.

Optional further reading
Matthew 11:25–30 (try *The Message* translation); Genesis 2:2–3;
Luke 10:38–42

Jesus washes **His disciples' feet**

'... he now showed them the full extent of his love.'
(v.1)

One Maundy Thursday, my mother was taking part in the traditional feet-washing service at church. 'I must wash my feet before I go and put them on display in front of everyone,' she remarked!

These days, the washing of the congregation's feet is a purely symbolic gesture, but not so in this story of Jesus. Interrupting His meal, He takes on the role of a servant to perform a less than pleasant task. In the preceding days, He and His friends had walked almost 100 miles along dusty roads from Galilee to Jerusalem for the feast. Their feet would have been extremely dirty.

Working as a volunteer in Kenya I had no car, so I would walk everywhere in open-toed sandals. The roads were poorly made and full of dust, which would turn into seas of mud when it rained. The dirt and dust became ingrained in my feet and, no matter how much I scrubbed them with a nailbrush, they rarely felt truly clean. Once, as a treat, I took myself for a pedicure. The therapist heated some water, added lavender oil, and invited me to soak my weary feet. She gently rubbed away the dirt and dust, and massaged in some foot cream in an attempt to soften the hard skin which had formed on my soles.

Earlier this month, we joined the disciples in recognising Jesus as the Son of God. Now let us unite with them once again, as we allow the Son of God, who created the world, to kneel as a servant and wash our feet. Let Him gently remove the dirt and dust that we would prefer others didn't see; let Him cleanse you and let Him love you.

For prayer and reflection

'**Meekness and majesty, Manhood and Deity, In perfect harmony, The Man who is God; Lord of eternity, Dwells in humanity, Kneels in humility, And washes our feet.**' **Graham Kendrick***

*Extract taken from the song 'Meekness and Majesty' by Graham Kendrick. Copyright © 1986 Thankyou Music

God cleanses Israel

Ezekiel 36:24–38

'... I will cleanse you from all your impurities and from all your idols.' (v.25)

For prayer and reflection

Lord, sprinkle me with clean water; forgive me, Lord; create in me a clean heart. Please send Your Holy Spirit to fill me and help me to do Your will.

The people of Israel had rejected God over and over again. They had turned away from Him to worship other gods and had indulged in evil practices. They had thrown out His laws and ignored His decrees. They had completely cut themselves off from God. But here, God tells the Israelites that He will bring them home; He will sprinkle them with clean water – an act of forgiveness. God promises them a new heart and a new spirit; they will be His people and He will be their God. He assures them of great blessings and fruitfulness; their land will become like the Garden of Eden (v.35). Then, and only then, will the people repent. I find the order of this sequence rather surprising – God's forgiveness precedes His people's repentance.

And what an amazing act of forgiveness it is. There are no half measures. God promises to restore their country, rebuild their towns and cultivate their land. More than that, He vows to place His very own Spirit to live within them. The Israelites had not asked for God's forgiveness and don't even deserve God's grace, but He gives it to them because He remains faithful to the covenants He has made.

I don't know about you, but if someone had hurt me that much I know that I'd find it almost impossible to truly forgive them. I might accept their apology; I may even say I forgive them; but my instinct would be to have nothing more to do with them – a form of self-preservation to avoid getting hurt again.

Our God is so amazing! After all this, He then went on to send His only Son to earth as a vulnerable child, and watched as we rejected Him yet again, this time letting Him die on a cross.

Clean hearts

Hebrews 10:19–25

'... having our hearts sprinkled to cleanse us from a guilty conscience ...'
(v.22)

Britain can seem a nation of compulsive washers. Supermarkets dedicate aisle upon aisle to cleaning products, guaranteeing a 'whiter wash' in order to fulfil our obsession with cleanliness. Expensive spa days, complete with luxurious treatments to cleanse our skin, have become increasingly popular.

There is nothing wrong with being clean on the outside. Yet all that external washing is in vain unless we change on the inside, deep inside our hearts. We tend to tuck things away to the back of our minds – those niggling little thoughts of things we have done or not done; things we regret doing or not doing. 'I wish I hadn't done that ... but no one knows, so it's all right.'

Of course, God knows everything we do; and if we have a guilty conscience then it blocks our path to God. How can we draw nearer to God in faith if our guilt acts as a barrier to the intimacy we are offered?

The solution comes in the Person of Jesus, that great High Priest who has opened a new way for us, so creating a new path to God. All we have to do is to have faith in Him and let Him sprinkle our hearts with water in order to cleanse us deep within. Jesus' sacrifice upon the cross has removed all the old barriers – sin, veils and curtains – and has given us the supreme confidence to enter God's presence by faith.

If there is something on your heart, something that bothers you and pulls you away from God, then resolve to end this today. Open your heart to Jesus through prayer; ask for His amazing forgiveness and be ready to receive His grace and love. Be prepared to walk forward in confidence!

For prayer and reflection

Lord, You know me inside out. I am sorry for the things that keep me apart from You; forgive me and sprinkle my heart with Your cleansing water.

John **the Baptist**

Matthew 3:1–12

'I baptise you with water for repentance.' (v.11)

For the third time this month, we find ourselves by the banks of the River Jordan, as it runs through the desert of Judea. John the Baptist must have cut quite an intimidating figure, with his camel hair clothes, his basic diet and his blunt way of speaking. Yet the people of the whole region came flocking in their crowds to see him – young and old, rich and poor, male and female.

I imagine that being baptised in the water by John was a nerve-wracking experience for them all. Given what we read of him, he was unlikely to have been that gentle with those who came forward! Yet fearfully they lined up and waited to be plunged into the flowing waters of the Jordan.

Try to place yourself in that mass of people; maybe you have travelled a long distance to be there. Be ready to move forward when it is your turn and you are called into the river by the wild-looking man before you. Imagine him taking a strong hold of you and sweeping you deep under the fast-flowing waters. For a few seconds, all you can sense around you is full immersion in the water; you feel disorientated and terrified. Then, once again, he pulls you upwards and you emerge soaking, spluttering and gasping for breath.

As you surface from the darkness of the swirling water, you can see the sunlight above you and feel the sun's warmth on your skin once more. This is your moment of rebirth, a time of redemption. Through this act of baptism, you have risen up out of the waters as a new-born infant (John 3:3–8), having washed away your old sinful life and been granted a clean slate and a fresh start.

For prayer and reflection

Read on in Matthew 3 for the baptism of the One without sin, the One who needed no repentance – the baptism of Jesus.

The baptism **of Lydia**

Acts 16:11–15

'The Lord opened her heart ...' (v.14)

Philippi was a Roman colony with few Jews and no synagogue. Instead, a place of prayer existed by the river. Lydia however, was a Gentile businesswoman, a dealer in purple cloth – what was *she* doing at the river?

Lydia was 'a worshipper of God'. She had not been raised in the Jewish faith, yet she had a strong sense of God; so much so that she went to the river to worship. Lydia was open to God, and then God opened her heart even more, so that she responded to Paul's words and was baptised by him.

Paul believed that once a person was baptised, he or she was clothed with Christ (Gal. 3:27). Through baptism in the river water, Lydia allowed the Holy Spirit to enter her receptive heart; clothed with Christ, she continued to be open to God's plan for her life.

After the baptism of Lydia and her household, she invited Paul and his friends into her home. We know that Paul planted a church at Philippi, and revisited the people there during Passover (Acts 20:6). It was a house church, meeting in one of the believers' homes – maybe in Lydia's house? As a successful businesswoman, she probably had a larger house than many. In addition, Lydia offered her home to Paul as a base, and a sanctuary after he and Silas were let out of prison.

What we do know for certain is the great love Paul had for the church at Philippi of which Lydia was a founder member. He referred to them as the 'saints' in his letter, and was undyingly grateful for their gifts to support his ministry (Phil. 1:3–5).

God achieves amazing things if we keep our hearts and minds open and receptive to Him.

For prayer and reflection

Lord, open my heart to Your voice; take my life and use it for Your glory.

The Monster Within

Brian Greenaway was president of a Hell's Angel chapter. He was violent, full of hate, deeply into drugs. Then, in Dartmoor Prison, he became a Christian, and life changed dramatically for him.

In the 30 or so years that have followed, Brian has not only faced and prayed through many of his own internal struggles and grown into a man of faith, but he has also introduced thousands of prisoners to Jesus, and set them too on the road to restoration and hope.

The Monster Within book and DVD are the result of many months of praying, hoping, planning and writing, as Brian has sought to encourage all those who have experienced rejection in their lives – in any one of many forms. His own experiences of being bullied, rejected by his family, seeking self-worth and comfort in a life of drink and drugs, and failing to find an answer to the monstrous feelings inside him, led to his coming to a faith in God that has seen him changed from a 'monster' to a 'missionary'!

Book
ISBN: 978-1-85345-740-1
£8.99 (excl. p&p)

DVD
EAN: 5027957001404
£10.99 incl VAT (excl. p&p)
Order now for mid-May delivery.

WEEKEND

Time to trust

For reflection: Psalm 27

'The LORD is my light and my salvation – whom shall I fear?' (v.1)

Volunteering in Kenya, I was suddenly taken seriously ill and rushed into hospital. My body seemed to shut down, there were so many things wrong with it. Apart from the physical pain I was feeling, I was terribly scared. And it was when I was at my very weakest that I felt God's presence most strongly, and learnt to trust in Him.

I was far from home, but I was never short of visitors. One memorable day, I was visited by a group of Maasai women in their beaded dresses, who had walked literally miles to reach the hospital.

I had difficulties sleeping, and would stay awake into the night, reading several favourite psalms over and over again, gaining a sense of peace. The nurses were very kind and one told me that they were praying for me.

I was concerned about coping on my own with the long flight back to the UK for convalescence. I need not have worried. A friend of a fellow volunteer was travelling on that same flight and was a registered nurse, so I was in safe hands.

God's strength and not mine.

Optional further reading
Isaiah 12:1–6; Matthew 19:13–15; Luke 8:40–56

Water from **the rock**

I f you have ever had to refrain from eating and drinking in preparation for an operation or medical procedure, then you can empathise with the plight of the Israelites – a dry tongue, a nagging thirst and an overwhelming desire for cold water.

When I lived in Kenya, nothing beat drinking cool water on a sweltering hot day after walking long distances on dusty tracks. I experienced an overwhelming feeling of relief as the refreshing water trickled down my throat. Without water, neither people nor animals will live very long.

As a community new to travelling, the Israelites found their situation unsettling after their relative security, albeit as slaves, in Egypt. In the hot, arid and unwelcoming Sinai desert, they quickly became scared and insecure. In their fear and anxiety, the Israelites lost their trust in Moses and their faith in the Lord. They became ungrateful and hostile.

It's easy for us to look at the Israelites and think that we would have kept the faith. But would you have joined in the moaning? Honestly? How often do we allow daily burdens, financial worries, stresses, family issues and job problems to get on top of us? Do we perhaps even blame God for our situations sometimes? It's not wrong to cry out to God for help in times of trouble. What we shouldn't do is to blame Him when things go wrong and then start to grumble.

'Be joyful always; pray continually; give thanks in all circumstances ...' (1 Thess. 5:16–18). Paul had been beaten, tortured and imprisoned for his faith; he was finally killed for it. Yet he gave thanks in every circumstance. Let us do likewise.

For prayer and reflection

I was taught this by a missionary friend in Chile – even if you've had the worst day, do not go to sleep until you have counted ten things for which to thank God.

Water **into wine**

John 2:1–11

'Fill the jars with water.' (v.7)

A wedding is a joyful time, but organising a special event like this is stressful. The bride and groom want it all to be perfect; yet there's so much to do, it's understandable how it is easy to miss one detail and not order enough wine!

Sheer human error made this bridegroom miscalculate the number of guests and the amount of wine required, and he found himself in a seriously embarrassing and dishonourable predicament. This mistake would not just blight their wedding day, but their married life together. It would bring shame on the bridegroom and his family in front of the whole community and his new wife's family – what did it say about his ability to provide in the future?

Fortunately for him, Jesus is a guest at the wedding. Like many of Jesus' miracles, it is not intentional; He does not schedule His 'good works'. Instead He just comes across people, like the blind beggar and the men with leprosy, who need His help. In fact, Jesus is 'off duty', relaxing and enjoying time with His friends. Yet He has compassion on the bridegroom's situation and, in a quiet and unassuming manner, He performs a miracle, for which He takes none of the credit.

We too need to do good when we see an opportunity to respond to other people's needs. This may well happen when we are either very busy or trying to relax; yet mission and service cannot be scheduled, and may well intrude on our personal time.

Jesus takes the ordinary (water) and transforms it into the extraordinary (wine). Let us give God our regular, daily lives and let Him turn them into something special and holy for His service.

For prayer and reflection

Lord, take my ordinary life and let me be holy for You, able to respond to those around me when and where they need my help.

Isaiah 55:1–13

'Come, all you who are thirsty, come to the waters ...' (v.1)

For prayer and reflection

'If anyone is thirsty, let him come to me and drink. Whoever believes in me, as the Scripture has said, streams of living water will flow from within him' (John 7:37–38).

Water **for the thirsty**

Water sellers in the ancient world would cry out to encourage thirsty people to purchase their water from them. Even today, fresh drinking water is bought and sold: in the UK we pay water rates; in the developing world water is still sold by the jerry can. But here, God is offering the exiled Israelites His water, wine, milk and food for free. Not only that, He presents the best; not some average meal, but 'the richest of fare' (v.2), and with no price tag attached.

Deported to Babylon, the Israelites felt cut off from God and His blessings. Their thirst was spiritual rather than physical. Thankfully, God did not forget His people and brought them back into His fold once more.

Just as He did for the exiles, God wants to give us water. He longs to quench our spiritual thirst, yet He does not believe in force-feeding! The water may be free, but we have to be ready to swallow what is on offer. If we drink His water, He will make an everlasting covenant with us: of His 'faithful love' as promised to David.

The passage ends with an image of fertility, as the earth bursts into fruitfulness and prosperity – no more thorns and weeds, but fertile, productive trees and plants. This is a vision of the good life God promises us all. If we are exiled from God, there is something missing in our lives. When we are united with God, we feel completed.

Is something holding you back from enjoying God's banquet, with its unlimited food and drink? How can you become an honoured guest? The answer is simple. Let Jesus, the Son of God Himself, invite you in. He offers us the water of life.

Water **for sharing**

H ave you ever knocked over a drink and watched the liquid spread? A little drop of water can go an awfully long way!

The continuation of Jesus' ministry after His ascension was not just left to 12 men. We have many accounts of people who received healing or help from Jesus who then told other people: the demon-possessed man (Mark 5:18–20) and the man healed of leprosy (Mark 1:40–45), amongst others.

Not only did the Samaritan woman gladly accept Jesus' offer of the water of life, she shared it with many of her compatriots, who believed in Jesus because of her testimony. It is not surprising that she was such a good evangelist – she'd learnt from the Master Himself.

Jesus gives us the blueprint for mission – a perfect example of how to do it right. Firstly, He meets with the woman in her own surroundings, where she feels at home. He engages with her, actually asking her for something – a drink. He doesn't preach at her; instead he holds a conversation with her and sparks her curiosity, using her questions as an opportunity for further teaching. He offers her something good, something positive, rather than berating her for her faults or judging her. It was not the done thing for a man to talk alone with a woman but, as always, Jesus reaches out to the people who need Him the most, regardless of their social status.

If you've received living water, the gift of eternal life from Jesus, then don't just keep it to yourself. This precious water is for sharing with others. Go, follow the example of Jesus and the Samaritan woman, and splash it around a little more.

'... the water I give him will become in him a spring of water welling up to eternal life.' (v.14)

For prayer and reflection

Dear Lord, please give me the opportunities to share Your living water with those who need it the most.

Thirsting for God

Psalms 42–43

'As a deer longs for a stream of cool water, so I long for you, O God' (42:1, GNB)

I t never ceases to baffle me how complicated we can make Christianity appear. Different faith traditions, church splits and schisms – these can seem complex, confusing and downright off-putting to an outside observer. Ironically, the essence of Christianity could not be simpler. Jesus encapsulated our faith into two straightforward commands: 'Love the Lord your God with all your heart and with all your soul and with all your mind' ... 'Love your neighbour as yourself' (Matt. 22:37–39). This is the very core of Christianity. It transcends all dogma, tradition, ritual, any of our good deeds and our many words. If our desire is not to love God with our whole being, then everything else is just meaningless.

Just as a deer being hunted under the hot sun longs for a stream of cool water, to restore her strength and give her a chance to save her life, so we should long to be with God and to love Him completely and absolutely. Without water, the deer will die. Without loving God, our life has no meaning.

In exile, the psalmist feels far from God. He used to be a leader of the Temple processions, a man of some status, but now he thinks that God has forgotten him whilst his enemies mock him. However, he cannot completely give up his hope in God, and ends on a note of optimism: he longs to worship once more in God's house.

We're more fortunate than the psalmist, as we do not need to go to the Temple or to any specific place to worship the Lord; we do not need to be with others to praise Him. We can love our God any time, any place, anywhere. All that matters is that we do so with our whole being.

For prayer and reflection

Lord, I love You more than words can ever express. I love You with my heart, strength, mind and soul.

WEEKEND

Time to pray

For reflection: Psalm 5

'I pray to you, O LORD; you hear my voice in the morning ...'
(vv.2–3, GNB)

Like many women, my mornings are quite rushed. A colleague, mum to two small children, commented that she often feels that she's done a whole day's work before even reaching the office!

Frequently, it seems impossible to find quiet time or space to spend in prayer first thing, but we really need to dedicate our day to God and receive the Holy Spirit. Then we can expect to experience those 'kingdom moments', which come from a daily reconnection to God; and even shine as a light for those around us.

I realised that I actually have several chances to spend a few minutes with God as I go about my daily morning routine. Sometimes I pray just before I open my eyes from sleep; sometimes I pray whilst in the shower; sometimes I pray on the station platform. Instead of making excuses to myself, the key thing is to get on and do it!

Consider your early morning opportunities to spend time with God in prayer. Look up and sense His presence. Note the colour of the sky and thank Him that the sun rises anew every morning. Receive His peace and carry it with you throughout the day.

Optional further reading
Mark 1:35–39; Daniel 6:1–28

....

Ezekiel 47:1–12

....

'... so where the river flows everything will live.' (v.9)

Water **from the Temple**

E zekiel the prophet paints an amazing series of pictures for us: the greatness of the Temple, the life-giving stream of water, the abundance of fish and fruit.

This is no ordinary river; rather it is a miraculous body of water. Firstly, the river does not follow the laws of nature. Instead its healing powers transform the extreme saltiness of the Dead Sea into fresh waters that sustain a vast array of fish, providing a plentiful source of food for the people who live along its banks. If that were not enough, these folk enjoy the goodness of fresh fruit of many kinds all year round. Amazingly, there is no need to wait until fruit comes into season; instead the trees produce a crop every month. It seems the more the fruit is harvested, the more it grows.

Secondly, neither does the river obey the laws of physics. The stream grows from a tiny trickle into a deep river too wide to cross, without any other waters adding to it.

This remarkable water behaves just like love. Love is not restricted to the laws of time or space. Love knows no confines. Love grows as it is needed. The more love you give away, the more love you have.

During her second pregnancy, my friend Tessa worried about how she could love another baby as much as her first child. But, of course, at the birth of a second baby, parents do not divide their existing love in half between their two children! Tessa discovered this when baby Olivia arrived; her love grew twofold to encompass Simon and his new little sister.

....

For prayer and reflection

....

Lord, I open myself to Your abundant and miraculous love. May it sustain me always.

Water **brings forth fruit**

'... like a tree planted by the water ... ' (v.8)

Last winter I planted a small apple tree in our garden. With no leaves, it seemed little more than a bundle of bare branches. However, it took root, reached deep for water underground and, in the spring, it blossomed. I hope to harvest some apples later this summer!

Just as my apple tree dug deep to let the transforming power of water flow within it, we too must open ourselves to the transforming power of God's Spirit. The Holy Spirit works in us, through us and with us, in a number of ways. The Bible, like the stream in these verses, is a key source of water to feed our minds and hearts. God's response to our prayers is like the rain, watering the dry land. Meeting and sharing with other Christians is like dew on the grass in the early morning, keeping us green and shiny. Even in times of spiritual drought, we will not fail to bear fruit if we have remained steadfast to Jesus, and allowed his Spirit to permeate every aspect of our lives.

Just as the roots of my apple tree are buried unseen beneath the ground, the Holy Spirit is not visible to the naked eye. Yet the consequences of letting Jesus work in our lives should be evident to everyone we meet.

There is a fruit for every season. In summer, watermelons refresh us and prevent dehydration; whilst, in winter, the vitamin C of oranges boosts our immunity against illness. The fruit of the Spirit is equally sweet, juicy and ripe. Paul promises that those who live by and are led by the Spirit will have love, joy, peace, patience, kindness, goodness, faithfulness, gentleness and self-control (Gal. 5:22–23). This is a harvest worth waiting for.

For prayer and reflection

Lord, I pray that You fill me with Your Holy Spirit. Without You, I am just a tiny seed, hard and dry. Water me and bless me, so I may bring forth fruit for You.

God pours out **His blessings**

'... I will pour water on the thirsty land, and streams on the dry ground ...' (v.3)

Here, God pours out three things: water on a dry land, His Spirit on the Israelites' offspring and blessings on their descendants. Just like water, blessings flow: they are poured out, they can be showered upon us, and they nourish and sustain us in dry times.

Sometimes Christians are accused of using their religion as a crutch to lean on. But there are no guarantees of special treatment when you become a Christian. Christianity is not a magic wand that will make you rich, happy and healthy! In fact, Jesus told His disciples: 'If anyone would come after me, he must deny himself and take up his cross daily and follow me' (Luke 9:23).

Life still has its challenges and difficulties to be faced. So where do the blessings fit in? The difference is that we are not on our own. God is with us. He sent His Son Jesus to die for us. His Spirit lives within us. 'And surely I am with you always ...' Jesus told His disciples (Matt. 28:20). Being a Christian gives meaning to our lives; we are the beloved children of God and members of His kingdom. We are no longer alone, as God loves to be involved in our daily lives and desires for us to be part of His bigger plans for His world.

The most beautiful aspect of being blessed by God is the opportunity to bless Him in return. Blessings do not simply flow in one direction. In verse 5, the people respond to God and swear allegiance to Him in a variety of ways. We too take the Lord's name; the word 'Christian' literally means 'little Christ'. When we worship, we praise and bless our God. We recognise His presence in our lives and give thanks for His grace.

For prayer and reflection

Lord, I want to shower my blessings upon You. I love You so much. I thank You that You give each day meaning and purpose. I love You, Lord Jesus.

Eternal life with God

'... he will lead them to springs of living water.' (v.17)

We started this month's reflections with the story of creation in Genesis, and we have come full circle to God's new creation in the book of Revelation. Water was present at the very beginning; and its presence is equally important in John's amazing vision of heaven for the people of God.

On a practical level, there is water for washing and drinking. There will be no more hunger or thirst in heaven. There will be no more pain and suffering. Jesus, the Good Shepherd, will lead them to springs of living water. There will be no more hurt or sadness, as God Himself will wipe the tears from their eyes.

On a spiritual level, the water of heaven represents so many of the themes we have considered over this last month: water for purification, for healing, for baptism and for blessing. Water is a symbol of eternal life with God, promised to all those who believe in His Son (John 3:16).

In the later chapters of Revelation, John uses vivid imagery to describe the last days on the earth, when no more rain falls (11:6) and the rivers dry up (16:12). But he ends triumphantly with his vision of a new heaven and a new earth. The New Jerusalem of the final chapter is home to the 'river of the water of life, as clear as crystal, flowing from the throne of God' (22:1). Water, a pure, clean, life-giving force, illustrates many of the characteristics of heaven and of God.

Next time you drink a glass of cold water, or listen to the sound of the rain, or take a warm shower, or see a river in full flood, remember that you are having a tiny foretaste of heaven.

For prayer and reflection

O God, thank You for the promise of eternal life with You. Cleanse me, heal me, bless me, Lord. Please make me fit to enter Your presence and stand before You.

Going for Gold

With the 2012 Olympic Games fast approaching, CWR introduces two new publications to spur you on in the race of life, as well as a summer programme of training to build your spiritual muscles!

Keep up the training

CWR has recognised that of the many people visiting the UK for the Olympic Games, there will be some who would like to take the opportunity to visit our headquarters and training centre, Waverley Abbey House, only a one-hour train ride from London Waterloo. Whether you live in the UK, or are a visitor – to enable you to make the most of a visit to us, we have arranged a full and varied programme …

Woman to Woman
Mon–Fri 16–20 July
This unique course is designed for women of all ages who want to help and minister to other women, whether on a one-to-one basis, leading a small group or with responsibility for a church or area-wide group.

Refreshing your View of the Bible
Mon–Fri 23–27 July
This course will give you an understanding of the overall message of the Scriptures, how God has used the authors to communicate His truth and, crucially, what it says to us in the twenty-first century.

Introduction to Biblical Care and Counselling
Mon–Fri 13–17 August
If you have a heart to help others but are wondering how, then this five-day foundation course is ideal. You will be helped to reflect on your own life in the light of the biblical model presented, before using the principles to help others.

Come for one week or all three!
For full details of the courses above/ to book, visit www.cwr.org.uk or call +44 (0)1252 784719

Inspiring champions

The first of our new publications is a devotional book entitled *Gold*. Richard Daly has written 100 inspirational thoughts on taking part in the race, the journey, which is our Christian life.

Gold by Richard Daly
ISBN: 978-1-85345-665-7
£4.99

Next is **Professor Bumblebrain's Absolutely Bonkers Champions**!

The star of our much loved **Professor Bumblebrain** series of children's books is back, this time with a full-colour comic on what it takes to become a true champion for God.

Professor Bumblebrain's Absolutely Bonkers Champions by Andy Robb
ISBN: 978-1-85345-656-5
£8.99 per pack of 10

Shining bright

We hope that something in this offering of publications and resources will appeal to you as you consider your own Christian 'race' or how you can reach out to others with the good news of Jesus.

Ideal for church and group resources

To buy visit www.cwr.org.uk/store or a Christian bookshop.

My times, God's timing

Psalm 31:1–9, 14–24

'But I trust in you, O LORD; I say, "You are my God." My times are in your hands …' (vv.14–15)

David, the shepherd boy, considered too unimportant by his father to be invited to the sacrifice with the prophet Samuel, is a most unexpected choice of future king (1 Sam. 16:1–13). But he is God's choice. After being anointed by Samuel, 'the Spirit of the LORD came upon David in power' (v.13). So begins a long (and surely difficult and confusing) wait. David only ever has honourable intentions to serve the current king, Saul, and proves his courage and faith in God by defeating the Philistine champion. But he's forced to live on the run to escape Saul, who is intent on murdering him.

Even when fleeing for his life, David trusts that his 'times' and life circumstances are in God's hands, waiting for God's timing to become king. One particular incident stands out for me. David and his outlawed men are hiding from Saul's army when Saul seeks the privacy of the same cave 'to relieve himself'. (Imagine teaching that story to six- to nine-year-old boys, as I tried to recently!) Despite his men's urging, David refuses to kill Saul, insisting that he will honour God's anointed king (1 Sam. 24:1–22). He will only become king himself in God's sovereign timing – however long it may take.

What an example! David believed that God knew everything about him, had ordained every day of his life (Psa. 139:16) and that God's timing was perfect – however irrational that timing might appear. Yet he was honest with God about his frustration too!

Join me this month as we delve further into the topics of time, seasons and God's ultimate timing. I pray that you'll be blessed, challenged and encouraged as we do.

For prayer and reflection

Lord, may I learn to trust, as David did, that 'my times' are truly in Your hands. Help me to understand more of Your ways and Your timing in my life.

WEEKEND

Resting in God

For reflection: Matthew 11:28–30

'Come to me, all you who are weary and burdened, and I will give you rest.' (v.28)

I wonder if you've recently heard (or said): 'If only there were more hours in the day – or days in the week!' Do we reach our weekend with a list of unfinished tasks, feeling that there's really not enough time to rest? Sadly, many of us do – at times, me included. Yet our Sabbath rest is commanded by God for our good (Deut. 5:12–15). For the Israelites the holy Sabbath gave them permission, as ex-slaves, to rest – something unknown beforehand.

I'm fascinated by God's provision of manna in the wilderness (Exod. 16). The day before the Sabbath God told the Israelites to prepare a double quantity (that exceptionally and miraculously did not go mouldy overnight) in order to rest on the Sabbath. God intervened supernaturally in His provision of manna; can He also do so with our time?

Just as those who tithe find that somehow their remaining finance is enabled to 'stretch' further (see Mal. 3:10), can we trust that, as we come to Jesus and rest (in whatever way is appropriate for us on our 'Sabbath'), the Lord will 'multiply' to us our remaining time to enable us to achieve what truly *must* be done?

Optional further reading
Exodus 16
Jani Rubery, *Time – Life Issues Bible Study* (Farnham, CWR: 2009)

Learning **from the Master**

**Matthew
3:13–4:11**

'And a voice from heaven said, "This is my Son, whom I love; with him I am well pleased."' (3:17)

Jesus is our model in everything – including His use of time. Let's consider three important factors as He begins His ministry:

i) Jesus knows who He is: the Son of God. This truth anchors Him, so when tempted with doubt by Satan: 'If you are the Son of God ...' Jesus doesn't entertain it, countering Satan's words with Scripture.

ii) Jesus knows that He is deeply loved and that God is pleased with Him (cf John 8:29).

iii) Jesus is empowered by the Holy Spirit (Matt. 3:16), only doing what He sees the Father doing (John 5:19).

Jesus' use of time is deliberate and purposeful. Often busy, with urgent demands upon Him, He appears unhurried and can say 'no' to needs and take time to rest (Mark 6:31). He doesn't burn out, but offers life and peace to others – from the same source He draws on daily, God's Holy Spirit (John 4:10–14).

So what can we learn from Him? In my own experience, I use my time most fruitfully when I'm feeling secure in my relationship with God – not feeling the need to please others or justify myself – and when I'm truly seeking the Spirit's guidance and empowering throughout my day. How about you? Try to answer the following questions honestly:

Do I know that God is smiling at me, His dearly loved daughter, today? When doubts creep in, do I resist Satan's lies and declare truth instead (eg Zeph. 3:17)? Am I filled with the Holy Spirit today, using the gifts He has given me, wherever I am, whatever I'm doing?

How we use our time will be crucially affected by who we believe we are – and whose power we are living in.

For prayer and reflection

Father, please burn in me the truth that I am Your deeply loved, precious daughter. May I sense Your smile and pleasure today. Empower me with Your Holy Spirit, I pray.

The tyranny **of the urgent**

I love being creative, socialising, serving, studying ... often filling my days to the full. Seeking to be fruitful, I'm aware of the dangers of procrastination and over-busyness. Yet my greatest challenge, as faced constantly by Jesus, is the 'tyranny of the urgent'. Urgent need can be overwhelming, making it impossible to focus on other important priorities. So, motivated by compassion, we respond constantly to urgent 'needs', ignoring our own vital requirements of rest and time alone with God to be refreshed, renewed and refocused, and eventually we 'burn out'. I've done this.

We read here that Jesus is able to step back from the urgent demands for healing to find solitude and time with God for prayer – and in so doing discern clearly His priorities: in this case to move on to somewhere new, leaving needy people behind. How can we learn from Him?

The crux seems to be able to discern, with God's help, the difference between the urgent and the important. One extreme example from Jesus' life: Jesus delayed going to see His dying friend Lazarus (after receiving an urgent plea for help) to do what was God's will and much more important – raise Lazarus from the dead (John 11). We may never have such a dramatic choice to make, but nonetheless we need His wisdom to discern how to prioritise our time. Sadly, much of it can be spent on the urgent but not important tasks in life, so sacrificing the non-urgent but most important. What priority do we put on prayer and time alone with God? Ask the Lord to show you any 'urgent' demands that are not actually yours to meet.

Mark 1:29–39; Luke 5:12–16

'... crowds of people came ... to be healed ... But Jesus often withdrew to lonely places and prayed.' (Luke 5:15–16)

For prayer and reflection

Spend time with God today evaluating the most important things in your life and the proportion of time you are devoting to them.

A sense **of timing**

John 12:20–36

'Jesus replied, "The hour has come for the Son of Man to be glorified."' (v.23)

Let's look at one final aspect of Jesus' use of time: His amazing sense of timing. Throughout His supernatural teaching and healing ministry, His comments reveal that He is conscious of God's preordained timing of events. Jesus carries out His Messianic purposes on earth with an awareness that timing is critical, beginning with His declaration in the Nazareth synagogue that He is to fulfil Isaiah's Messianic prophecy: 'Today this scripture is fulfilled in your hearing' (Luke 4:21). Subsequently certain decisions on timing baffle His disciples: for example, as we saw yesterday, instead of going immediately to heal the dying Lazarus Jesus 'stayed where he was two more days' (John 11:6), knowing that the miracle of raising Lazarus from death would bring the greatest glory to God.

From Jesus' words recorded in John's Gospel, we see that He knows His life on earth will end unnaturally prematurely; and that, in addition to establishing God's kingdom on earth, He has come to die as a sacrifice for the forgiveness of sin and to overthrow the works of Satan. 'Now is the time for judgment on this world ...'; 'Jesus knew that the time had come ...'; 'Later, knowing that all was now completed ... Jesus said, "It is finished." With that, he ... gave up his spirit' (John 12:31; 13:1; 19:28,30). As He dies, Jesus knows that He has completed what He has come to earth to do; His mission accomplished.

For prayer and reflection

Lord, I have given You my life. Help me to hear and obey You in the minutes and hours of my days.

Can you remember when you last experienced a sense of critical timing in your own life? 'For we are God's workmanship, created in Christ Jesus to do good works, which God prepared in advance for us to do' (Eph. 2:10).

Always

**1 Thessalonians
5:16–24**

'Be joyful always;
pray continually;
give thanks in all
circumstances, for
this is God's will
for you in Christ
Jesus.' (vv.16–18)

Writing to the Thessalonian Christians, the apostle Paul emphasises the importance of living in continual relationship with God. But how do we pray continually when immersed in a demanding job or hectic family life? Be joyful always? Brother Lawrence, a lay brother in a 17th-century monastic community, gives us insights into how he practised being aware of God's presence at all times – whether working in the kitchen or worshipping at church. For him there was no distinction between the two. Jesus had told His disciples: '... surely I am with you always ...' (Matt. 28:20), and Brother Lawrence took the Lord at His word, writing to his friend:

'... think often of God, by day, by night, in your business, and even in your diversions. He is always near you and with you; leave Him not alone. You would think it rude to leave a friend alone who came to visit you: why then must God be neglected? Do not then forget Him, but think on Him often, adore Him continually, live and die with Him ...' *

Brother Lawrence believed that the Lord wanted to be involved in every aspect of his daily life, however mundane. Do we believe that too? Do we find moments to chat to Him, knowing that He is longing to hear our voice, and to listen to Him over all the other competing voices in our day? Do we ask Him to fill us daily with His Holy Spirit? Can we spend a few minutes each day, however trying or difficult it has been, remembering the good things we can be thankful for? These habits will bring us closer to the Lord, allowing Him to permeate our days with His presence and our lives with His light and life.

*Brother Lawrence, *The Practice of the Presence of God* (Oxford: Oneworld Publications, 1993) p.65.

For prayer and reflection

Lord, help me to be conscious that You are always with me and that You want me to turn to You and hear Your voice. I long for a deeper relationship with You.

'Just in time …'

Acts 12:1–19

'The night before Herod was to bring him to trial, Peter was sleeping … an angel of the Lord appeared …' (vv.6–7)

Peter, awaiting trial, knows that James has just been executed. Yet he seems not to be having an anxious, sleepless night. In spite of chains, and guards surrounding him, he's so soundly asleep that the angel strikes him on his side to wake him up. As believers are praying, Peter is miraculously freed from prison – just in time. No wonder he thinks he is dreaming; certainly Rhoda can't take it in!

Perhaps you've also experienced God's 11th-hour timing, in provision, healing or 'deliverance', as I have. Asleep in the passenger seat of our car on a long late-night journey with my father, I heard an urgent voice: 'Carol! Carol! Wake up!' Seconds later our car failed to take a bend, heading for a high brick wall; my father asleep at the wheel. I wrenched it round, averting disaster … saved, by an angel?

But what about those who are not healed or delivered from death? John the Baptist, Stephen and James were martyred – as are many Christian brothers and sisters today. Corrie Ten Boom, imprisoned during World War II in Ravensbrück concentration camp where her beloved sister Betsie died, retells an incident from her childhood:

'… I went to my father and said, "Daddy, I am afraid that I will never be strong enough to be a martyr for Jesus Christ." "Tell me," said Father, "when you take a train trip … when do I give you the money for the ticket? Three weeks before?" "No, Daddy, you give me the money … just before we get on the train." "That is right," my father said, "and so it is with God's strength. Our Father in Heaven knows when you will need the strength … He will supply all you need just in time."'*

*From a letter written by Corrie Ten Boom in 1974.

For prayer and reflection

Lord, when I'm desperate for You to act, may I trust that You'll be there 'just in time' – to heal me, provide for me, deliver me or give me all the strength I need.

WEEKEND

Too much time on your hands ...

For reflection: Genesis 39:20–23

I love the story of Joseph: in the most extreme circumstances he surrendered himself totally to God. Joseph spent 13 years altogether in captivity (firstly enslaved, then imprisoned) before his meteoric rise to power as Pharaoh's prime minister. What was his attitude during those difficult years? It seems that in no way did Joseph turn against God or blame Him for his unjust circumstances. He was aware of God's sustaining presence with him, for we read: '... while Joseph was ... in the prison, the LORD was with him; he showed him kindness and granted him favour ...' (vv.20–21).

Thousands of Christians today worldwide are suffering persecution – many unjustly imprisoned, like Joseph. Wang Mingdao, a famous Chinese evangelist, imprisoned for 20 years, mostly in solitary confinement, said: '... I had nothing to do ... except get to know God. And for 20 years that was the greatest relationship I have ever known.'*

This weekend, pray for those in prison that they too would get to know God – either for the first time or, if imprisoned for their faith, that God would strengthen them in their suffering, grant them His favour and enfold them in His love. For further prayer points, see www.opendoors.org

Optional further reading
If time, why not read Joseph's entire story: Genesis chapters 37; 39–50?

*Source – Open Doors. Used with permission.

Waiting **and heartache**

Luke 1:5–25,
39–41,56

'Both of them were
upright in the sight
of God … But they
had no children …
and … were both
well on in years.'
(vv.6–7)

**For prayer and
reflection**

**Lord, when I
don't understand
what You are
doing in my life,
please give me
the grace to
remain strong
in trust and hope,
and faithful
to You.**

Elizabeth is one of my Bible heroines. This godly woman must have suffered so much throughout her early married life. The stigma of childlessness (believed then to be a curse from God) hung over her; and she a descendant of Aaron and married to a priest! What was her hidden sin? How the neighbours must have speculated. At the very least she would have been the object of sympathy or pity.

But here's the rub. I believe it's possible that Elizabeth suffered, in part, because in God's plan it was not yet time for her 'miracle son' to be conceived. Mary, her relative, might desperately have needed the encouragement of another 'supernatural', God-initiated birth at the time of Jesus' conception by the Holy Spirit. She was only a teenage girl, while Elizabeth was 'in her old age' (Luke 1:36). So Elizabeth lived through these long barren years while Mary grew up; and, on their joyous reunion, the baby inside Elizabeth leapt at the sound of Mary's voice!

What a precious three months they must have spent together – praying for each other, preparing for their sons' births. Did Elizabeth help Mary through the early days of morning sickness? Did they make children's clothes together? I'm sure there was a very special bond between them.

So what can we learn from Elizabeth? In her time of waiting and suffering she remained a godly, faithful, worshipping woman – a perfect mother for her supremely important prophetic son. Don't allow your pain and suffering to turn you away from God. Look at Elizabeth, draw strength from her example – and trust in God's goodness; as she did, through her pain.

God **breaking in ...**

"or my thoughts are not your thoughts, neither are your ways my ways," declares the LORD' (Isa. 55:8). Did Isaiah's words perhaps cross Mary's mind after the angel Gabriel left her to take in his unexpected news?

This week as we continue to consider how God's supernatural timing affects our lives – at times cutting across our plans – we realise how vividly Mary must have experienced this. A young betrothed teenage girl, full of hopes for her future married life, the last thing Mary expected would be to find herself in such a dangerous predicament. She'd submitted herself totally to God's will and timing, but what would her parents and Joseph make of this mysterious pregnancy? Would they believe her story? They must – everything, her life itself, depended on it! (See Deut. 22:23–27.)

We know, with hindsight, that the Lord, in His amazing love for Mary, chose her, a virgin, to fulfil prophecy concerning the Messiah's birth (Isa. 7:14). He knew her love for Him and His purposes, and her obedient, servant heart – she would be the perfect mother for His precious, beloved Son.

Other biblical figures – Moses, Gideon, Samuel, even shepherds – experienced God breaking supernaturally into their day (or night). So might we. As Philip Greenslade writes: 'But when you do glimpse Him or hear Him, it will not be to enrich your stockpile of spiritual sensations but to implicate you further in the ongoing story of God's plans to bless and save the world.'* Mary willingly submitted to the Lord's timing and plan for her life. How will we respond, if He breaks into our day?

*Philip Greenslade, *The Big Story* (Farnham: CWR, 2010) p.236.
**Ibid, p.237.

"'I am the Lord's servant," Mary answered. "May it be to me as you have said.'" (v.38)

For prayer and reflection

'If God were to call you to do something for Him today, are you there – listening, eager, willing and ready to do His bidding?'**

What's worrying you today?

Is it your health? Your finances? Your family? Jesus knows our frailties, says **Elizabeth Rundle**, and He outlined a complete antidote to worry for us

' Therefore I tell you, do not worry about your life, what you will eat or drink; or about your body, what you will wear ... Each day has enough trouble of its own' (Matthew 6:25-34).

It sounds as though the disciples had been fussing! These 12 men had taken a momentous step to become disciples of Jesus, relinquishing their jobs and walking away from their homes. Is it any wonder that the enormity of what they had done was causing them anxiety? After all, which of us, after taking a life-changing decision, has not wrestled with those niggling doubts when the first burst of enthusiasm has subsided?

Maybe it had dawned on Peter, James, Matthew and the others that life as an itinerant disciple was not quite as rosy as they had expected and, at times, seemed full of uncertainties and insecurity.

Sometimes they were a long way from the nearest village and food supply ... What on earth were they going to eat? They were moving around the countryside – their clothes wouldn't last forever – they would need 'better' garments for going up to Jerusalem, and leather boots for winter ... All these valid concerns were evidently sprinkled through their conversations.

Jesus heard their worries and knew that His men, just like us, could win medals in the art of worrying. So, when He went up on the mountainside and sat down to deliver the famous teaching that we call the Sermon on the Mount, He incorporated a special word for the worriers.

Over the past two decades, I've visited the Holy Land in several different seasons, and it has been marvellous to sample the variety of weather and scenery with which our Lord would have been familiar. Until very recently, however, I'd never been in Galilee in February.

Wild flowers dotted the landscape in multicoloured clumps of yellow mustard, scarlet anemones, white daisies, violet Maltese Cross flowers and wild irises mingled with many other indigenous plants. It made me think that perhaps it was early spring when Jesus gave this teaching. Seated on the hill in warm sunshine overlooking the Sea of Galilee and surrounded by a glorious natural carpet, He used 'the lilies of the field' as the perfect visual aid (Matthew 6:28–29).

I love to watch the swallows constructing their nest with only a beak and two little feet. Their instinctive ingenuity and skill leave me spellbound.

Jesus used those simple sights, which are common the world over, to open His disciples' eyes of faith. If God has created the birds and flowers with such loving care, how much more will He provide and care for us?!

In the context of life and death, peace and war, hunger and thirst, clothes would come under the heading of 'trivia'. The disciples did not need to be overly concerned about such matters ... Worry grabs us all at some point in our lives ... but when worry takes a stranglehold on our lives it destroys our capacity to live in the present moment. Worry can become literally disabling and, when it takes such a hold, then God is pushed away.

The disciples had food and they were clothed, but they were projecting their worries into the future. Too much focus on the future, and what might go wrong in it, can taint our gratitude of the present.

Jesus asked, 'Why do you worry ...?' Our grateful thanks go to Matthew for enabling us, two millennia later, to read the words of Jesus addressing our worries today.

This article first appeared in full in *Woman Alive* (June 2008), Britian's only Christian magazine specifically for women. Used with permission.

God's **delays**

Matthew
1:18–25

'… he had in mind to divorce her quietly. But after he had considered this, an angel of the Lord appeared to him …'
(vv.19–20)

One detail that puzzles me is why God revealed His plans to Mary and Joseph at different times. The angel Gabriel first spoke to Mary. God could have also arranged Joseph's dream, confirming His plans for the virgin birth, on the very same night. Then, when Mary and Joseph recounted their supernatural encounters, they'd have been able to reassure one other. But in God's divine wisdom it did not happen that way.

Joseph 'had in mind' to divorce Mary privately, to avoid public disgrace. This means that Joseph knew of her pregnancy, yet did not, or could not, believe the explanation of divine conception. It had never happened before – so why should he? *The Nativity*, shown by the BBC, vividly portrayed the emotional turmoil the betrothed couple might have endured during this agonising period. Faithful, loving Mary, desperately wanting to be believed; Joseph, confused, furious, heartbroken at her betrayal. So why did God allow this delay?

Likewise, with hindsight, we know why Jesus delayed setting off to heal the dying Lazarus, but for Mary and Martha the few days between Lazarus' death and his being raised to life were unbearably painful: days of grief, confusion and anguish (John 11:1–45).

There may be no obvious reason to us as to why God sometimes allows delays. God's ways and timings are not ours. Perhaps you are currently living through one such delay. Like Mary, the mother of Jesus, and Mary and Martha before us, let us hold on to the knowledge of God's perfect love for us and His unfailing goodness.

For prayer and reflection

When everything in me cries out for You to act and yet Your answer seems delayed, help me to cling on to the fact that You are utterly trustworthy and good – and You truly love me.

How much longer, Lord?

Luke 2:21–40

'Sovereign Lord …
you now dismiss
your servant in
peace. For my
eyes have seen
your salvation …'
(vv.29–30)

A s the nativity story unfolds we read this wonderful account of Mary and Joseph taking the baby Jesus to be presented to God at the Temple. Keen to obey the Law for Mary's purification (Lev. 12:1–8), they bring with them the sacrifices required from those too poor to be able to afford a lamb – a pair of doves or pigeons.

Inside the Temple that day are two elderly servants of God – Simeon, a devout, righteous man, and Anna the prophetess, aged 84, widowed after only seven years of marriage. The Holy Spirit had revealed to Simeon that he would see the Messiah before he died. Did he expect the Messiah to come in the form of this tiny baby, I wonder, born to such a poor couple? Or was he expecting someone more mature and authoritative? How important it was that Simeon heard the prompting of the Holy Spirit, both in leading him to the Temple at that time, on that particular day, and also in recognising the Christ in the form of Jesus. How much time must he have spent in prayer, waiting on God, listening to His voice, in the intervening years? Did he wait patiently? Did years pass uneventfully before God prompted him that day? We're simply not told.

Whether you're very young (see 1 Sam. 3), older, a new Christian, have known the Lord for 80 years, or anything in between, God wants you to hear His voice. If He makes a promise to you a period of waiting may be involved and the shape of the answer may not come exactly as you expect. But stay tuned to the Spirit: however old you are, your most significant act of obedience or service to the Lord may yet be to come!

For prayer and reflection

Lord, thank You for Your faithfulness in keeping Your promise to Simeon. Help me to learn to discern Your voice and the prompting of Your Spirit when You speak to me.

....

Acts 8:26–40

....

'So he started out, and on his way he met an Ethiopian eunuch, an important official …' (v.27)

Right place, **right time**

I'd like to continue looking at the importance of being sensitive to the Lord's voice in order to be used in His timing. Philip, as we read today, hears the voice of an angel telling him to take the desert road and arrives just as the chariot of a high-ranking Ethiopian official passes by. On God's prompting, Philip approaches the chariot, just as the man is struggling to understand Isaiah's prophetic words. Invited to climb into the chariot, Philip gently explains the good news of Jesus and, minutes later, baptises the eunuch as a new believer in the Lord.

You may never have experienced such a timely or dramatic encounter; you may now even be permanently housebound. May I suggest that our physical weakness is no limitation to the Lord if we are open to follow His promptings and pray.

Years ago I was part of a church-planting team in inner-city Marseille. One day we were due to present an evangelistic drama on the quayside. Having suffered a recent burnout, I explained to the Lord that the most I could manage was to go and watch, sitting on an adjacent bench – could He then draw people to me with whom He wanted me to talk? I will never forget the humbling and precious hour spent sharing from the Bible and praying with an elegant older lady. She had decided to take a final walk into town before committing suicide that day – so much was she grieving the loss of her late husband. The Lord knew her route, where she would stop and sit and with whom she would be able to share her tears and pain. The woman left having rediscovered a childhood faith in God and knowing that He loved her.

....

For prayer and reflection

....

Lord, whatever my circumstances, please make me sensitive to Your voice to be in the right place at the right time – to share Your love with others who need You.

WEEKEND

Time to stop ...

For reflection: Luke 10:25–37

'But a Samaritan, as he travelled, came where the man was; and when he saw him, he took pity on him.' (v.33)

It was Sunday morning, so I set off across Norwich by car to arrive at church in good time. En route I noticed an Indian man standing in the pouring rain beside a car full of passengers (including children), attempting to hitch a lift. Unusually, as I was travelling alone, I decided to stop. Visitors from Nottingham, they'd run out of petrol and had no idea of where the nearest petrol station was. 'Jump in,' I said, 'I'll take you.' I'd be late for church, but I'd read the Parable of the Good Samaritan that very morning – as I laughingly explained to the man as he apologised for delaying me. Waiting in the rain for an hour, he estimated that 60 cars had passed without stopping. I was challenged ... Our lives can be so time-pressured, our diaries so full that we no longer have the time to stop ... or do we?

Likewise, our Sundays (often seen as our Sabbaths) can be both busy and stressful (church rotas, Sunday lunch, entertaining, visiting family ...). In his excellent book *Ordering Your Private World**, Gordon MacDonald suggests that, if this is true for us, we might need to look at booking extra space into our diaries to simply stop.

Optional further reading
Luke 10:38–42; Psalm 23:1–3; Deuteronomy 5:12–15
*Gordon MacDonald, *Ordering Your Private World*, (Nashville, Thomas Nelson, 2003)

A time **for everything**

Ecclesiastes 3:1–8

'There is a time for everything, and a season for every activity under heaven …' (v.1)

This week we focus on a different aspect of God's timing: times and seasons for different activities of life. King Solomon, a man of 'wisdom and very great insight' (1 Kings 4:29), wrote these words, but years ago I couldn't see how they related to me. When would I make war (v.8), for example? Yet spiritually I have: battling, through prayer and fasting, for breakthrough for a person or situation, followed by laying down the outcome and resting in God's peace – even with the issue seemingly unresolved.

Rob Parsons of the charity Care for the Family speaks of the importance of enjoying each stage of family life. 'Make the most of reading those bedtime stories to children when they're young, for there'll come a time when you'll pick up that familiar, well-loved storybook and they'll say: "Not tonight – that's babyish."'* Phases of life pass quickly.

At times the Lord prepares us for the next step. I once felt prompted to devote an evening a week to clearing out cupboards (I don't enjoy this so I put off starting it). Months later the Lord called me to overseas mission work and I had to rent out my house quickly. How I wished I'd obeyed the prompting! Boxes of unsorted papers followed me for years, moving from loft to loft!

So, what may the Lord be speaking to you about? Making time to invest in your children, nieces, nephews, friends or elderly relatives? Time for decluttering, making space for the new? Time for study, rest or renewal in Him? Make the most of this time in your life as it won't last forever.

For prayer and reflection

Heavenly Father, please make me aware of what is especially important for me to invest time in right now. Thank You that you care about *every* aspect of my life.

*Rob Parsons, Chairman and Founder of Care for the Family. Used with permission.

A time **to laugh**

'... a time to weep
and a time to
laugh, a time to
mourn and a time
to dance ...' (v.4)

The title of a recent *Woman Alive* article intrigued me: 'Does God have a sense of humour?' When babies are born chuckling and smiling, and the sound of children's laughter fills many a playground, why do we need to ask the question? We are made in God's image! But do we really believe He created laughter too?

For centuries Christians have battled an image of unsmiling dogmatism, of being 'killjoys' ... and yet the Bible is full of exhortations to be joyful. Moreover our bodies are created in such a way that laughter is both infectious and also releases endorphins that reduce stress and promote wellbeing. It even helps to prevent heart disease. Laughter is good for us!

Tomorrow we'll read the precious words, 'Jesus wept'. How I wish there were an equally short verse stating: 'Jesus laughed!' Isaiah tells us that Jesus was 'a man of sorrows, and familiar with suffering' (53:3) and so Jesus is often portrayed as serious and intense. Didn't He ever laugh? Seeing *The Life of Christ* performed at Wintershall in Surrey brought many aspects of Christ's story vividly to life but none more so, for me, than His sense of humour. As 'Jesus' and His disciples danced, Jewish-style, in the Cana wedding scene, He was laughing, joking and having fun! Why hadn't I ever seen Jesus in that way before?

Do we, as Christians, sometimes take our life and calling so seriously that we risk squeezing out even those essential times of laughter with our friends? Is life stressful or challenging for you? God created laughter, and 'A cheerful heart is good medicine ...' (Prov. 17:22). Let's enjoy His gift as often as we can.

For prayer and reflection

Lord, fill me again with the joy of my salvation – and may the joy of Your Holy Spirit bubble up within me. Thank You for the gift of laughter.

A time **to mourn**

Matthew 5:4;
John 11:1–6,
17–27,32–36

'Blessed are those
who mourn,
for they will be
comforted.'
(Matt. 5:4)

'Time heals', we hear, but my husband, whose mother died 33 years ago when he and his brothers and sister were young, would disagree. They still bear the scars of having buried their grief and never having mourned healthily together.

Jesus tells us that those who mourn will be blessed and comforted. Mourning strikes me as active, not passive, involving remembering, talking about, crying over ... which takes time. Sadly, nowadays little time is given to those who are grieving. Life carries on regardless. After a bereavement or loss (of a loved one, friendship, career or dreamed-for family), we have to pick up the pieces, move on and act as normal ... Or do we?

A few years ago our church leader and his wife suffered the tragic, unexpected loss of their younger son, James. Working alongside him, I'd see his door firmly closed at lunchtime. He told me that he'd look at photos of James, listen to James's music and allow time, alone with God, for his grief to surface – before resuming his day. At night he and his wife lit a candle in James's memory to remember him together. I've learned much from their example.

We may not all be able to deal with our grief in this way but the principle remains. To mourn a loss takes time. The apostle Paul exhorts us to 'mourn with those who mourn' (Rom. 12:15) as shared grief binds us closer, allowing us to strengthen and comfort one another. How precious Jesus' tears must have been to Mary and Martha – expressing His love for them and their late brother, Lazarus. If you are currently mourning a loss, may you too know the Lord's love, compassion and comfort in your grief.

For prayer and reflection

Father, You promise to comfort all who mourn and grieve. Be especially close to .... May they, and I, know Your loving embrace holding and comforting us as we mourn.

A time **to feast**

Psalm 36:5–9

'They feast in
the abundance of
your house; you
give them drink
from your river
of delights.'
(v.8)

My parents, evacuees during World War II, married during a time of rationing in the 1950s. Family members donated clothing coupons to buy the material for my mother's homemade wedding dress, and people learned to live on very little. As a student, I too learned to make meals 'stretch', and in my twenties I adopted the slogan, 'Live simply, that others may simply live'.

Yet on studying the Jewish feasts and festivals I was struck by their lavishness and abundance. Apart from Christmas dinners at home, the concept of 'feasting' was quite unfamiliar to me. So it surprised me when I hit upon a particularly expensive and lavish idea to celebrate my parents' joint 70th birthdays: a minibus would take them, plus brothers, sisters-in-law and closest friends, to a 'Big Band' dinner dance at the famous Savoy Hotel in London. My sister agreed, and it was the most enormous success. The venue and food were exceptional and everything went perfectly – my parents, who loved this style of music and dancing, and knew nothing in advance, were absolutely overwhelmed!

Little did we know then that within just over a year both our wonderful mother and uncle (her brother) would have died ... I now strongly believe that God prompted us to organise that surprise celebration – and at just the right time.

As you meditate on today's verses, ask the Lord to reveal new truths to you about feasting on Him and His Word; about experiencing His lavish generosity and abundance of love. How better can you express His generosity and abundant love? When did you last make time to feast and celebrate?

For prayer and reflection

Lord, You turned water into wine so that the wedding feast at Cana could continue. May I learn to feast in Your house – and express Your generosity to others.

A time **to fast**

Matthew 6:16–18

'When you fast, do not look sombre as the hypocrites do …' (v.16)

For several years I fasted regularly on Thursdays. So when, one Monday, I awoke feeling that I should fast I was surprised. 'It's not Thursday today', I thought, dismissing the idea. This happened the following day, and the next … I explained my confusion to a friend. 'Perhaps God's telling you to fast,' she said simply. Why hadn't I thought of that?

So I began to fast, not knowing how long the fast would last. Drinking fluids, but replacing meal times with prayer, worship and Bible study, I worked, cycled, even ran up and down stairs – perfectly healthy and well. Five days later I considered starting to eat again, but didn't want to lose the closeness I was experiencing with the Lord, so ate one light meal at lunchtime, fasting morning and evening, for a further five days. On Day Ten I felt prompted to declare: 'Lord, I'll do whatever it takes to get the effects of Satan out of my life!'

The following Sunday the speaker challenged us to become more vulnerable to others. Vulnerability was a 'dirty' word for me – smacking of weakness and dependency. 'Go forward for prayer,' the Lord said. I froze – then remembered my words. I had no choice – and so began a transformation in my relationships with both God and other people.

I don't fully understand the spiritual power in fasting. However, I know that we're given clarity, spiritual perception, our prayers become more effective (Mark 9:28–29), the Holy Spirit speaks and God's will seems to be done on earth.

Might God be telling you that it is time to fast …?*

For prayer and reflection

Father, I long to be fully free to serve You. Please reveal to me what is holding me back and teach me how to fast and pray.

*If you've never fasted before, begin slowly, perhaps missing just one meal – reading the Bible and praying instead. If you are pregnant, breast-feeding, on medication, underweight or have diabetes, consult your doctor first.

JUL/AUG 2012

July

JAMES AND JUDE

CHRISTINE PLATT

August

PSALM 34 – TASTING THE GOODNESS OF GOD

HELENA WILKINSON

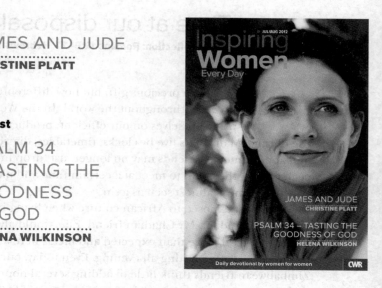

In **July**, Christine Platt challenges us with the forthright writing of Jesus' brothers, James and Jude, to see whether our own actions match the faith we confess.

In **August**, Helena Wilkinson explores Psalm 34 – a psalm of praise, hope, trust, instruction and deliverance – encouraging us to experience God's goodness as David did.

Obtain your copy from CWR, your local Christian bookshop or National Distributor. If you would like to take out a subscription, see the order form at the back of these notes.

WEEKEND

Time at our disposal ...

For reflection: Romans 12:9–21; Hebrews 13:1–2

Time is such a precious gift, but how differently it is perceived throughout the world. In the West we pride ourselves on our efficient, productive use of time. Many of us live by clocks, timetables, diaries and appointments. Friends may no longer just 'drop in' on each other – they plan to meet at a certain time and place. 'Wasting' time is almost seen as a sin.

I was first exposed to African culture when living in France as a student. My Chadian friend, Elie, would always cook for several more than expected and meals were a rolling affair, often lasting all evening. Even today, our Zimbabwean friends think little of adding several hours to their journey to re-route in order to visit us, even if for only an hour, before their six-hour return home. Time is at their disposal; relationships are more important.

Multi-tasking is a 'women thing' – but can we become so obsessed with 'making the most of our time' that we sacrifice quality for quantity? Relationships take quality time, concentration and emotional energy. Do we run the risk of becoming slaves of time? Doing more and achieving less?

May the Lord open our eyes to show us what we can learn from other cultures.

Optional further reading
Genesis 18:1–15
Lynn Penson, *Seasons* (Farnham: CWR, 2011)

Seasons of life

**Song of Songs
2:11–13**

'See! The winter
is past ... Flowers
appear on the
earth; the season
of singing
has come ...'
(vv.11–12)

Wherever we live, God has created seasons
for us to enjoy: whether rainy, dry, spring,
summer, autumn or winter. As a child I
loved autumn. The russet, yellow and crimson tones of
the leaves enchanted me. Now spring is my favourite
season: after a long winter the sight of snowdrops
peeping through bare earth always thrills me. Winter
is over! Yet I am also more aware of the importance of
winter. As growth is halted above ground, the energy of
plants goes back into strengthening the roots.

It seems that our lives, too, can be 'seasonal'. Periods
of growth, vigour, new life and expectancy (like spring);
times of activity, pressure and 'heat' (summer/dry);
periods of change/letting go (autumn) and seasons
where all seems desolate, barren and hopeless (winter).
These 'seasons' are not age-related – I experienced my
first 'winter' at 22, in direct response to a prayer: 'Lord,
deepen my faith.' A lengthy period of agonising heart-
searching followed: every challenging question of my
atheist friends suddenly became a burning issue for me.
It was a deeply uncomfortable time. Only years later was
I able to say, like Job: 'My ears had heard of you before,
but now my eyes have seen you' (Job 42:5, NCV).

Are you currently facing 'winter'? Don't give up –
it will end, however long it has already lasted. Draw
nearer to others for their support; don't remain isolated
and vulnerable. The Holy Spirit has not left you – He
may be doing a much deeper work inside. Whichever
season you are in, God is equally present, truly God
with us – Immanuel – and will never leave us nor
forsake us (Heb.13:5).

**For prayer and
reflection**

**When I pass
through a winter
season, Lord,
please deepen
and strengthen
my roots in You –
and give me hope
that spring will
come again.**

Time **for some pruning?**

John 15:1–17

'... every branch that does bear fruit he prunes so that it will be even more fruitful.' (v.2)

Much as I love flowers I'm not a natural gardener – our small garden is proof! Backing onto woodland, it's packed with flowering shrubs and three over-large fruit trees, all jostling for available sunlight. It's been a constant battle to 'tame' it. Our attempts at pruning (at the wrong time or in the wrong way) have led to non-flowering lilac or forsythia or, worse still, apple trees shooting to the sky, devoid of fruit.

Jesus tells His disciples that we are like the branches of a vine that are expertly pruned by God the Father – at the right time and in the right way. Dead, unfruitful wood is removed, but note ... even the good, healthy, fruit-bearing branches are pruned right back. So how does this relate to our lives, I wonder? Might it not be just those things we've continued for years (not through faith, vision or desire, but simply because we can't say 'no') – the potentially dead wood – that God wants to prune away; but also perhaps the activities that are going well and we're passionate about ...?

Do you, like me, ever forget that fruit does not simply equate to 'activity' for God? The Lord does want us to bear *much* fruit, but the quality of the fruit is also supremely important. '... the fruit of the Spirit is love, joy, peace, patience, kindness, goodness, faithfulness, gentleness and self-control', the apostle Paul explains (Gal. 5:22–23).

Is it time for the Lord to do some pruning in your life? Listen to what He's saying to you and try to co-operate fully – then trust Him for the wonderful fruit to come!

For prayer and reflection

Father, it's hard when You seem to be stripping away something I enjoy. Help me to trust You and, by the power of Your Spirit working within me, increase Your fruit in and through me.

Where is my mindset?

Colossians 3:1–4;
Matthew 6:19–21;
2 Corinthians
4:7–18

'... store up
for yourselves
treasures in heaven
... For where your
treasure is,
there your heart
will be ...'
(Matt. 6:20–21)

'Oh no! I've just lost a reward in heaven!' my friend exclaimed, much to my surprise. She'd just told me, inadvertently, about an act of kindness and generosity that she'd intended to keep secret, as Jesus instructed (Matt. 6:1–4). This happened years ago, but she recently said that now, more than ever, she was increasingly conscious of eternity – and the importance of using her energies to work for God's eternal purposes. I was challenged to ask myself: 'Where is my mindset?'

The writer to the Hebrews tells us that the heroes of faith were 'aliens and strangers on earth' ... 'longing for a better country – a heavenly one' (Heb. 11:13,16). The apostle Paul frequently challenges us to live with eyes fixed on the eternal world: 'So we fix our eyes not on what is seen, but on what is unseen. For what is seen is temporary, but what is unseen is *eternal*' (2 Cor. 4:18, my emphasis). Likewise Jesus makes it clear that we should be storing up treasure in heaven – living our lives for eternal purposes, working not 'for food that spoils, but for food that endures to eternal life ...' (John 6:27). But how, practically, can we?

Sharing our faith and God's love by serving others is one obvious way; but the more 'hidden' disciplines of prayer, intercession and fasting are also powerfully used by God to affect eternity and will be rewarded (Matt. 6:5–6,16–18). Ask the Lord how He wants you to use or invest your particular gifts in His kingdom purposes and then follow His leading. How wonderful to be welcomed 'home' with the words: 'Well done, my good and faithful servant! Here is your reward.'

For prayer and reflection

Heavenly Father, may my life on earth count for eternity. Show me how best to invest my time and energy for the purposes of Your eternal kingdom.

Carpe diem!

Acts 16:16–34;
Ephesians
5:15–16

'Be very careful
… how you live –
not as unwise but
as wise, making
the most of every
opportunity …'
(Eph. 5:15–16)

**For prayer and
reflection**

**Could the Lord
be saying to you:
'Make the most of
the opportunities
I'm giving you
and allow Me to
stretch you to
bear fruit beyond
all you can ask
or imagine'?
Will you?**

What type of person are you? Are you an action woman or do you, like me, tend to procrastinate just that little bit too long, so missing the opportunity to act?

Two years ago, while visiting Zimbabwe, I was taken aback when congratulated on having reached such a good old age of … 50 (such is the tragic mortality rate in the country). This was in stark contrast to the '50 is the new 40' birthday cards I'd received at home. Was I taking my longevity for granted? Was I really valuing *every* day of my life? Fulfilling my calling? Making the most of God-given opportunities to use my spiritual gifts and share my faith?

Opportunities, by definition, have a limited lifespan. The apostle Paul also wrote to the Colossian Christians: 'Be wise in the way you act toward outsiders; make the most of every opportunity. Let your conversation be always full of grace, seasoned with salt, so that you may know how to answer everyone' (Col. 4:5–6).

Unjustly imprisoned in Philippi, Silas and Paul have been flogged and their feet shackled. So, at midnight, what are they doing? Bemoaning their woes? No, with a literally 'captive' audience they are praying and praising the Lord in front of the other prisoners 'listening to them'. When a supernatural earthquake occurs, breaking open chains and prison doors, Paul's quick and wise reaction prevents the jailer killing himself – and the amazing end result is the salvation of the jailer and his entire family!

'Carpe diem' – seize the day. What opportunities is the Lord giving you today? Will you take them?

Never too late to start again

....
John 21:1–19
....

'Then he said to him, "Follow me!"'
(v.19)

As we end this month, you may still be feeling discouraged. Perhaps years ago the Lord's voice seemed clear, His love more real. Disappointments, failures, even conscious disobedience, may have diminished your awareness of His presence. You no longer see yourself bearing fruit for Him. You're not alone. Peter must have had similar feelings after his humiliating denial of Christ (Luke 22:54–62). Yet Jesus didn't only love Peter on his good days, but unconditionally. He'd known this would happen, warning Peter in advance. Even the anguish on Christ's face as He looked at Peter may have expressed more than His own pain; He knew the torment His close friend would suffer.

And so, after His resurrection, a message was sent to Peter – encouraging him that he was still both loved and wanted as friend and disciple: '... go, tell his disciples and Peter, "He is going ahead ... into Galilee"' (Mark 16:7). When Jesus finally met Peter on the beach, He singled him out for a chat, and three times gave Peter the opportunity to restate his love. Jesus wanted Peter to know that in spite of His past mistakes He was still sought out and wanted – just as the father of the prodigal was looking out for his son to return (Luke 15:20) and later went after the jealous elder brother who needed reassurance of the father's love and affirmation of his place in the family.

If today you are feeling on the edge of God's family, questioning whether Jesus really still wants you as His disciple, these are His words to you: 'I love you and have always loved you. Follow me again – and leave the past behind. It's time for a fresh start.'

....
For prayer and reflection
....

Lord Jesus, thank You for the reassurance of Your love for me. I want to commit myself afresh to You and Your purposes for me. Please help me to make a fresh start.

WEEKEND

We'll praise Your name forever …

For reflection: Revelation 1:4–6; 5:11–14

'To him who sits on the throne and to the Lamb be praise and honour and glory and power, for ever and ever!' (5:13)

While on holiday in Cornwall my husband told me that experiencing the spectacularly beautiful coastline gave him 'a glimpse of heaven'. I've received such 'glimpses' while in worship: once, at Taizé, where Christians of many nations were worshipping God in one language (Latin), the sense of the Lord's presence and anointing was so great I was moved to tears. Worship and heaven seem almost synonymous to me.

But how do we prepare for an eternity of worship and adoration of our Lord? John, in his book of Revelation, presents images of the worship taking place in heaven, in which we'll share. However an eternity of worship begins here on earth. This weekend, as you spend time reflecting on these images, which characteristic of our Lord causes you most to love Him? Ask the Lord for a revelation of His glorious beauty and try to find a new way to express your worship. Offering our bodies 'as living sacrifices' is worship (Rom. 12:1); could you use yours in a new way: raising hands, dancing, lying prostrate, kneeling, jumping before the Lord?

In closing our month, please join me in worship:

'O come let us adore Him; for He alone is worthy; we'll praise His name forever – Christ the Lord!' Amen.

Optional further reading
Revelation 5:1–14; 7:9–17; Ephesians 3:14–21

ORDER FORM

5 EASY WAYS TO ORDER:

1. Phone in your credit card order: **01252 784710** (Mon–Fri, 9.30am–5pm)
2. Visit our Online Store at **www.cwr.org.uk/store**
3. Send this form together with your payment to:
   CWR, Waverley Abbey House, Waverley Lane, Farnham, Surrey GU9 8EP
4. Visit your local Christian bookshop
5. For Australia and New Zealand visit KI Entertainment at **www.cwr4u.net.au**

For a list of our National Distributors, who supply countries outside the UK, visit www.cwr.org.uk/distributors

YOUR DETAILS (REQUIRED FOR ORDERS AND DONATIONS)

Name: CWR ID No. (if known):

Home Address:

                                               Postcode:

Telephone No. (for queries):   Email:

PUBLICATIONS

TITLE	QTY	PRICE	TOTAL
Total publications			

UK p&p: up to £24.99 = **£2.99**; £25.00 and over = **FREE**
Elsewhere p&p: up to £10 = **£4.95**; £10.01 – £50 = **£6.95**; £50.01 – £99.99 = **£10**; £100 and over = **£30**

Total publications and p&p A [   ]

Please allow 14 days for delivery

SUBSCRIPTIONS* (NON DIRECT DEBIT)

SUBSCRIPTIONS* (NON DIRECT DEBIT)	QTY	PRICE (INCLUDING P&P)			TOTAL
		UK	Europe	Elsewhere	
Every Day with Jesus (1yr, 6 issues)		£15.50	£19.25	Please contact nearest National Distributor or CWR direct	
Large Print *Every Day with Jesus* (1yr, 6 issues)		£15.50	£19.25		
Inspiring Women Every Day (1yr, 6 issues)		£15.50	£19.25		
Life Every Day (Jeff Lucas) (1yr, 6 issues)		£15.50	£19.25		
Cover to Cover Every Day (1yr, 6 issues)		£15.50	£19.25		
Mettle: 14–18s (1yr, 3 issues)		£13.80	£15.90		
YP's: 11–15s (1yr, 6 issues)		£15.50	£19.25		
Topz: 7–11s (1yr, 6 issues)		£15.50	£19.25		
Total Subscriptions (Subscription prices already include postage and packing) **B**					

Please circle which bimonthly issue you would like your subscription to commence from:

JAN/FEB MAR/APR MAY/JUN JUL/AUG SEP/OCT NOV/DEC

* Only use this section for subscriptions paid for by credit/debit card or cheque. For Direct Debit subscriptions see overleaf.

CONTINUED OVERLEAF >>

‹‹ SEE PREVIOUS PAGE FOR START OF ORDER FORM

PAYMENT DETAILS

☐ I enclose a cheque/PO made payable to CWR for the amount of: £ _____

☐ Please charge my credit/debit card.

Cardholder's name (in BLOCK CAPITALS) _____

Card No. ☐☐☐☐ ☐☐☐☐ ☐☐☐☐ ☐☐☐☐

Expires end ☐☐ ☐☐　　Security Code ☐☐☐

GIFT TO CWR
☐ Please send me an acknowledgement of my gift　**C** ☐

GIFT AID (YOUR HOME ADDRESS REQUIRED, SEE OVERLEAF)

giftaid it

I am a UK taxpayer and want CWR to reclaim the tax on all my donations for the four years prior to this year **and on** all donations I make from the date of this Gift Aid declaration until further notice.*

Taxpayer's Full Name (PLEASE USE BLOCK CAPITALS) _____

Signature _____ **Date** _____

*I understand I must pay an amount of Income/Capital Gains Tax at least equal to the tax the charity reclaims in the tax year.

GRAND TOTAL (Total of A, B, & C)

SUBSCRIPTIONS BY DIRECT DEBIT (UK BANK ACCOUNT HOLDERS ONLY)

Subscriptions cost £15.50 (except *Mettle*: £13.80) for one year for delivery within the UK. Please tick relevant boxes and fill in the form below

☐ Every Day with Jesus (1yr, 6 issues)
☐ Large Print Every Day with Jesus (1yr, 6 issues)
☐ Inspiring Women Every Day (1yr, 6 issues)
☐ Life Every Day (Jeff Lucas) (1yr, 6 issues)

☐ Cover to Cover Every Day (1yr, 6 issues)
☐ Mettle: 14-18s (1yr, 3 issues)
☐ YP's: 11-15s (1yr, 6 issues)
☐ Topz: 7-11s (1yr, 6 issues)

Issue to commence from
☐ Jan/Feb ☐ Jul/Aug
☐ Mar/Apr ☐ Sep/Oct
☐ May/Jun ☐ Nov/Dec

CWR　Instruction to your Bank or Building Society to pay by Direct Debit　**DIRECT Debit**

Please fill in the form and send to: CWR, Waverley Abbey House, Waverley Lane, Farnham, Surrey GU9 8EP

Name and full postal address of your Bank or Building Society

To: The Manager ___ Bank/Building Society
Address _____
Postcode _____

Name(s) of Account Holder(s)

Branch Sort Code ☐☐ ☐☐ ☐☐

Bank/Building Society account number ☐☐☐☐☐☐☐☐

Originator's Identification Number　4 2 0 4 8 7

Reference

Instruction to your Bank or Building Society
Please pay CWR Direct Debits from the account detailed in this Instruction subject to the safeguards assured by the Direct Debit Guarantee.
I understand that this Instruction may remain with CWR and, if so, details will be passed electronically to my Bank/Building Society.

Signature(s) _____

Date _____

Banks and Building Societies may not accept Direct Debit Instructions for some types of account